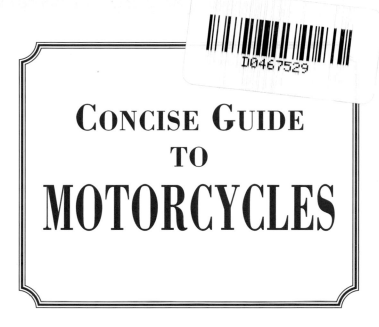

CONCISE GUIDE
TO
MOTORCYCLES

Text by
Franco Mazza

Grange
BOOKS

Published By Grange Books
An Imprint of Grange Books PLC
The Grange, Grange Yard, London SE1 3AG
Published 1994

Printed in Italy by Litostampa I.G. - Gorle
ISBN 1 - 85627 - 587 - 6

THE MOTORCYCLES

A HUNDRED YEARS OF MOTORCYCLES

Four wheeled vehicles have a great variety of practical uses and are ideal for transport or simply getting around, but right from the early days the motorcycle has always been the perfect manifestation of that wonderful sensation known as the "-thrill of speed".

You can get an idea of how dangerous and at the same time how exciting it was to ride a motorcycle from looking at photographs of the first races which took place at the beginning of the century. The roads, the dust, those primitive yet often incredibly powerful machines clearly evoke the sense of daring of the early enthusiasts.

All we have to recreate the atmosphere of those heroic days are faded photographs or the stories told by some old mechanic or perhaps a grandfather. But lucky for us, meetings of motorcycle enthusiasts are becoming more frequent so we can still experience some of the thrill of the early races or simply just admire the brilliantly polished old "-knights of steel".

This book takes a brief look at the development of the motorcycle. The photographs were mainly taken at recent meetings and races. These are interspersed with period adverts to give some idea of the kind of advertising used by the producers of the time.

Some readers may be able to recognize one of their own precious machines. To these readers I express my warmest thanks for their unknown collaboration.

It seems right to me to begin my brief survey of images with an advertisement taken from an old issue from the beginning of the century of the Italian

4

Touring Club Magazine. The illustration shows a bicycle and a motorcycle side by side. This highlights the origin of the motorcycle in the need of the cyclist for greater freedom of movement while at the same time making less effort.

There were of course other attempts to achieve the same thing, such as the steam powered tricycle. But this really belongs to the "sane lunacy" period of motoring history at the end of the last century when there were all manner of motorized vehicles on the roads.

The first races which took place illustrate the great variety. In the Paris - Bordeaux - Paris race of June 1895 there were four wheeled vehicles, tricycles and two motorcycles, a Hilderbrand and Wolfmuller and a Millet. Then at the Emancipation Run in 1896, the first ever London - Brighton race, all kinds of vehicles took part including a French Dalifol-Volta steam motorcycle.

There were a great many long distance races of this type with cars, tricycles and motorized bicycles all competing together right up until 1900.

At the beginning of this century, however, the

A BSA from the twenties. The fuel tank is particularly attractive.

Two ingenious solutions to the problems of suspension and headlamps.

various manufacturers started to abandon the more cranky versions of two wheeled vehicle and the modern motorcycle began to take shape.

In 1888 Felix Millet produced a bicycle with a radial five cyclinder engine fitted onto the rear wheel. But the problem of the awkward bulk of the "Otto cycle" engine was only resolved in the early years of this century. At the same time solutions were found to the other difficulties relating specifically to motorcycles: the relation between the engine and the cycle frame, the transmission system and the

braking mechanism.

This last problem tended to be undervalued in the beginning since the manufacturers were mainly interested in producing ever more powerful machines which were tried out on tracks rather than roads. This made the motorcycle more of a circus spectacle than a means of getting around on the roads. The Hildebrand and Wolfmuller had front

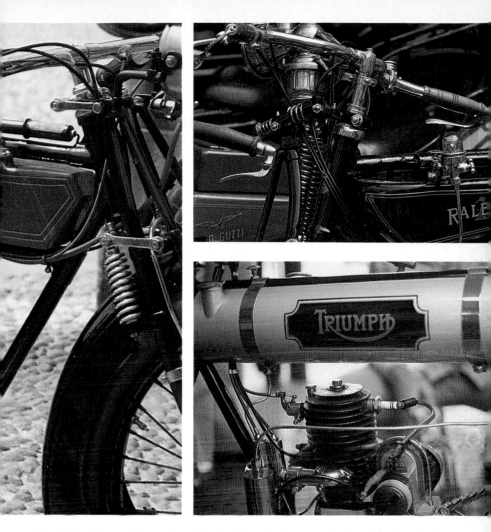

wheel brake pads and a kind of pedal operated emergency anchor which could be released to drag into the ground.

It was the Americans who in the early years of the century pioneered the development of the motorcycle as a road vehicle. Machines were produced which were especially designed to go at high speeds over unpaved roads with holes and stones.

The imagination runs riot in the design of engines, headlamps and fuel tanks, etc, producing a great variety of forms.

*Two cycles from
the twenties:
ROUGEMULTI
(Great Britain)
and INDIAN
(USA).*

To deal with these difficulties the cycle frames were strong and the engines very powerful, 1000 cc four stroke models. The Indian also used a half leaf spring of the kind found in motor cars.

The American machines were usually big, so it is easy to understand how they could easily become popular in Europe, where the motorcycle had not yet greatly distinguished itself from the bicycle.

At this time motorized bicycles were produced by a great number of manufacturers who very often made use of De Dion Bouton or Laurin and Klement engines.

It was necessary to produce motorcycles which combined the power and durability of the twin cy-

clinder American models with the lightness and manoeuvrability of the European motorized bicycles.

The English firms were the first to achieve this with their famous single cylinder engines. These were a great success in sporting competitions and names like Sunbeam, Norton and AJS son became well-known.

Typical features of the English machines were a single cylinder four stroke engine, separate gears and side drum brakes.

Road races such as the Tourist Trophy held on the Isle of Man became common all over Europe. Such

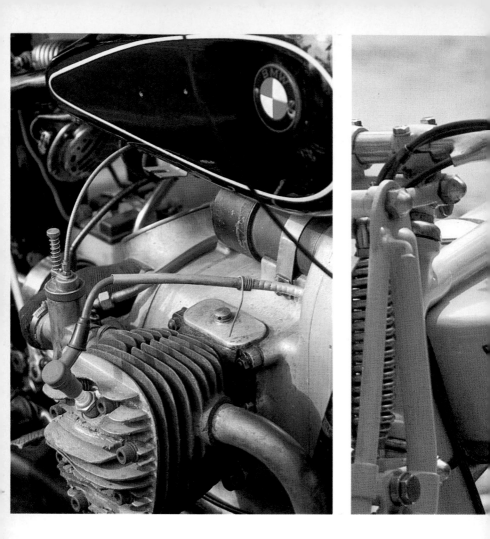

TWIN CYLINDER BMW with the revolutionary horizontal cylinders.

races had the obvious aim of showing an ever increasing public models which were very similar to normal mass-produced machines.

In the thirties the English manufacturers gained remarkable success. The Velocette of that period for example had a foot gear change control, rear suspension with a swinging arm fork and telescopic shock absorbers.

The Italian firm BIANCHI produced the famous "Blue Arrow" 350 in 1924. It was designed by M. Baldi.

During the same period progress was being made in Italy. In particular, names like Guzzi and Bianchi as well as Benelli and Gilera, just to mention the most famous, considerably improved the power and performance of their machines and achieved considerable commercial success.

In Germany the emphasis was on two stroke engines and BMW in particular perfected its famous

horizontally opposed twin, which clearly derived
from the motor car engine.

In Italy, too, multi-cylinder engines achieved
great success, especially after the second world war
with the twin cylinder Guzzi and the four cylinder
Gilera, Mv and Benelli.

After the war the English motorcycle began to
fall into decline in correspondence to the the Italian

producers' ability to diversify and create a wider range of two-wheeled vehicles such as the famous Vespa and Lambretta scooters. Diversification also occured in France, where a variety of mopeds became very popular, and in Germany where an enormous number of small makes and models sprang up.

It was only in the sixties that the Japanese entered

DELLA FERRERA 350 cc, 1932. In the thirties the Turin based firm produced technically advanced machines.

the picture. Up until that time they had been careful observers of all that the European motorcycle manufacturers produced.

Honda used multi-cylinder four stroke engines based on Italian models, to which however they made a few modifications, notably the use of four valves per cylinder. Yamaha, Susuki and Kawasaki opted instead for two stroke engines.

MOTO GUZZI normal model 21.

The Japanese paid particular attention to the frames and the braking systems. They abandonded the drum brake in favour of double disc brakes on the front wheel and a single disc on the rear wheel.

ARIEL 1930. This English motorcycle has a four cylinder engine of 497 cc, overhead camshaft and four-speed gears.

In recent years the Japanese have dominated the market for powerful machines. They offer value for money and nationwide technical assistance, something which the European producers have never been able to achieve.

At present we can see a revived interest in motorcycles and two-wheeled vehicles in general. There are numerous different models and types available for different purposes: for road, track, off-road and

GNOME

3 **CV** – Bloc |moteur
Type **E 3** – 250 cmc

RHONE

city. In meeting these current needs many European producers are enjoying considerable success.

The motorcycle is no longer a vehicle for those who cannot afford a motor car, as it was in the old heroic times. Today it is a machine to be enjoyed for its own sake.

ASTRIDE TWO WHEELS

Once it had appeared on the scene the motorcycle quickly spread throughout the whole world, with producers active in sport as well as manufacturing.

Here we present a brief history of this development as it took place in different countries.

France

It is right and proper to begin our survey of almost a century of motorcycle history, in both its

Advertisement from the French GNOME RHONE for the models of 1928.

The sidecar adds some of the characteristics of the car to the motorcycle. It finds its peak of development in England in the 1930s. Here we see a MOTO GUZZI with sidecar.

COUPE DE L'ARMISTICE (11 Novembre) - 1928 -

contrairement à certaines affirmations, ne partage pas sa place de 1er en Catégorie 350 cmc. avec d'autres concurrents, le résultat officiel est le suivant :

Catégorie 350 cmc.   **1er**   **COULON** sur Moto **TERROT**

- Seule Marque remportant la Médaille d'Or attribuée à cette - Catégorie et seul coureur pouvant prétendre au titre de premier.

Ce magnifique résultat obtenu dans une Catégorie qui ne comportait pas moins de 24 arrivants, est tout à l'honneur de la grande marque française et de sa fameuse 350 cmc.

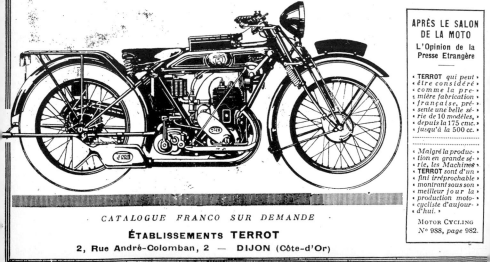

APRÈS LE SALON DE LA MOTO
L'Opinion de la Presse Etrangère

« TERROT *qui peut* » « *être considéré* » « *comme la pre-* » « *mière fabrication* » « *française, pré-* » « *sente une belle sé-* » « *rie de 10 modèles,* » « *depuis la 175 cmc.* » « *jusqu'à la 500 cc.* »

« *Malgré la produc-* » « *tion en grande sé-* » « *rie, les Machines* » « TERROT *sont d'un* » « *fini irréprochable* » « *montrant sous son* » « *meilleur jour la* » « *production moto-* » « *cycliste d'aujour-* » « *d'hui.* »

MOTOR CYCLING
N° 988, page 982.

CATALOGUE FRANCO SUR DEMANDE

ÉTABLISSEMENTS TERROT
2, Rue André-Colomban, 2 — DIJON (Côte-d'Or)

technical and human aspects, with France, the first country to get really serious about road racing and the production of motorcycles.

Count De Dion, his mechanic Georges Bouton, Felix Theodore Millet and before them Ernest Michaux were all Frenchmen whose ideas and experience were fundamental in the early development of the application of the internal combustion engine to a cycle frame. The brothers Eugenio and Michele Werner, although not French by birth adopted French nationality. In Paris they found the perfect environment for the development of their ideas, which finally led to the building of the first "motorcycle".

Already at the end of the last century France was seething with ideas connected with the new discoveries that were being made in mechanics and chemistry. They were exciting times, with the new scientific discoveries undermining the old belief that the problems of science had more or less been solved. Yet the discovery of new theories led to the need for them to be tried out personally. So it was that enquiring minds became pioneers of danger: the

Advertisement for the French TERROT *of 1928.*

Above, a "four-seater" MOTO GUZZI.

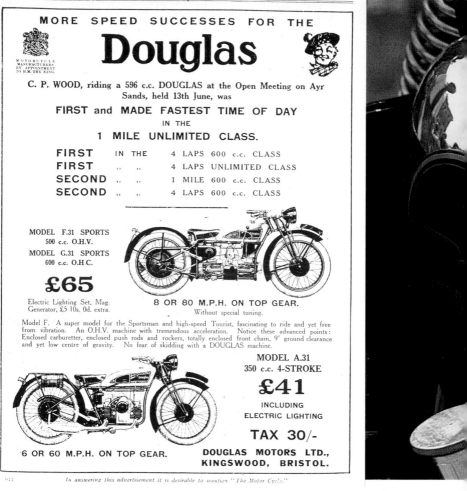

Advertisement from THE MOTOR CYCLE, *1931.*

Montgolfier brothers in the airballoon, Bleriot in the aereoplane, Marcel Renault in the car and Murice Fournier on the motorcycle. Even before these pioneers, in the the early 1700s Denis Papin had built a motor-powered paddle-wheel boat which crossed the river in the town of Kassel in Germany. Papin was a leading figure in the development of motorized transport, but his inventions

were not without their cost to him personally. The boatmen of Kassel, fearing to lose their work, attacked and destroyed his wonderful machine.

Coming back to the early 18s, when the airballoon had become reasonably safe and steam ships had been sailing for some time, the French turned their attention to three new vehicles: the aeroplane, the car and the motorcycle. Common to all three

Manufacturers adopt the latest techniques of design. MOTO GUZZI in 1938 employs an elastic frame.

ANNOUNCING a new 500 c.c. O·H·V

ROYAL ENFIELD

MODEL L.O.2

With the opening of the Spring Season comes another example of Royal Enfield organised efficiency—an attractive 500 c.c. O.H.V. at an equally attractive price. Backed by the vast resources of the Enfield Works, it possesses the mechanical perfection inseparable from all Royal Enfields, and has a wonderfully complete specification. Ask your local dealer to show you this remarkable new model.

The specification includes:—488 c.c. O.H.V. engine with **total enclosure of working parts**, dry sump lubrication; Lucas 6-volt combined lighting and ignition set with gear-driven dynamo and large capacity battery; **foot-operated four-speed gear;** duplex frame of great strength and rigidity having sidecar lugs incorporated; patent cush drive rear hub; Dunlop 26 × 3.25in. tyres, expanding hub brakes 6¼in. diameter; quickly detachable rear mudguard; Dunlop weatherproof saddle; large saddle tank finished aluminium with green panels; front fork has finger adjusted shock absorbers and steering damper; patent prop stand; etc.

CASH PRICE
MODEL L.O.2

£49.17.6
or by Gradual Payments.

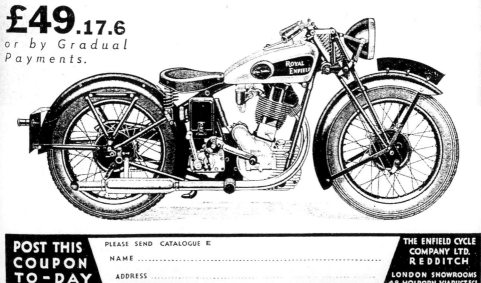

A19

In answering this advertisement it is desirable to mention "The Motor Cycle."

was the impossibility of relying on the tried and tested steam engine. Instead there were only the uncertainties of the "Otto cycle" engine.

So at the beginning the various developers and test drivers all relied on one another. Bleriot commissioned Anzani, a racer and builder of motorcycles, to make him a motorcycle capable of taking him as far as England. Fournier raced cars during

Advertisement for ROYAL ENFIELD, 1935.

MM, a company known for its technological inventiveness.

the same period in which he was thrilling the public on the cycle track. Soon afterwards, not content with the work of others, he began to build his own bikes, creating that terrific beast of the track that prompted a contemporary journalist to write, "No man can ride this machine without risking his life and limb!"

The English VELOCETTE, *which was the first to introduce the foot gear-change control, rear suspension with a swinging arm fork and telescopic shock absorbers.*

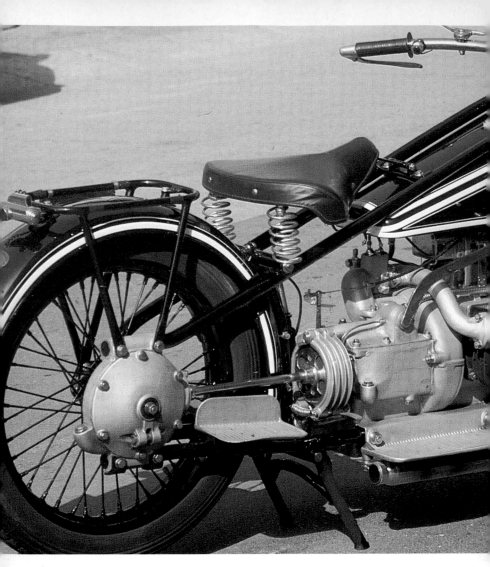

Great Britain

The English are well-known for being phlegmatic, not so easily excited as the Latin people and full of self-control. But all this is true only in normal conditions. When they sit astride a motorcycle, all their perfect self-control gives way to a crazy de-

Two models from BMW. This firm would reach the heights of motorcyle manufacturing producing technically high quality machines.

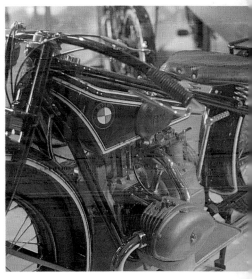

sire to race and defy the laws of balance and reason.

The English have always been particularly fascinated by motorcycles, perhaps because of their ancient love of riding thoroughbred horses over wild country and the battlefields of war.

In central Europe Czechoslovakia achieves fame as a motorcycle maker. Here we see a CZ.

Before the beginning of this century speedlovers on two and four wheels in Britain were held back by the strict laws which favoured the use of horse drawn vehicles. After the Emancipation Run, the English were able to get involved in motorcycle racing, which was easy to organize in that all you needed was a cycle track.

Racing was immediately a great success. All the craftsmen who already made their own individual if eccentric machines, as well as those who worked on a larger scale producing such wonderful bikes as Raglan, Rudge and Triumph, became better organized and seriously set about making motorcycles.

A SUNBEAM with sidecar.

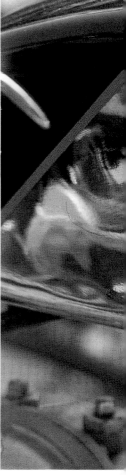

The main centres of production were Coventry, Wolverhampton and Birmingham, which were the homes of such legendary names as Norton, Rudge, Triumph, Matchless, AJS and, last but not least, Sunbeam.

Common features of all the early models produced in England were their brilliant performance and mechanical strength, making them the equal of the big American twin cylinder machines.

Right from the start the English motorcycle makers produced competition models that dominated the most important sporting events in Europe. Later, however, when it became more demanding both technically and financially to take part in races, Norton, AJS and Velocette, the big names in English motorcycles, gradually withdrew from competitions. They were convinced that the high quality of their mass produced machines would be

By the forties the motorcycle had become an attractive looking machine. The English MATCHLESS and the Italian SERTUM are two fine examples.

sufficient to make up for the loss in publicity which they gained from taking part in world championship races. It proved to be a great mistake. English motorcycle manufacturers had always incorporated modifications and improvements tried out on the race track. And it was this that had enabled them to gain such commercial success.

Germany

If France has the merit of being the country which put motor racing on the map, and if England and America developed the motor industry, Germany is no less important in its contribution to the development of the steam and internal combustion engine with such figures as Daimler,

Otto and Diesel.

It was Otto and Langen who got the motor industry going in a really big way and saw the enormous potential for the engines they had developed. Some time after Hilderbrand and
Wolfmuller they connected an Otto cycle engine
to a sort of bicycle and tried, with somewhat more

difficulty, to build up a large commercial organization in order to exploit their ideas before others could catch on.

Despite the enterprising initiative of the two partners from Munich, the motorcycle industry in Germany was actually caught off balance by the machines made by the Werner brothers and their various imitations which they had to deal with as soon as their motorcycle appeared on the European market.

A few years later, however, in Neckarsulm, NSU, a firm which until 1873 had made knitting machines, began to make a name for itself for the excellent quality of its bikes, which it began making in 1900.

Models used for military purposes are more robust and especially designed for off-road use. Here we see a HARLEY DAVIDSON *and a* BIANCHI.

The front mudguard is used for name plates and motifs evoking speed.

For the Germans precision was an absolute necessity, and mechanical engineering, in which each bit of the mechanism had to fit exactly with every other and with the whole in order to work at optimum efficiency, seemed to offer them the perfect means of expression and give them an outlet for the national passion for efficiency.

Italy

Italy has a well founded tradition in the development of the internal combustion engine. This tradition was begun by Eugenio Barsanti and Felice Matteucci, who were the first people in the world to patent a device which produced mechanical power through the explosion of a gas.

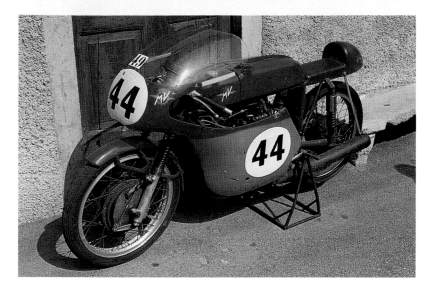

After the initial theoretical-experimental phase, which ended really with the construction of the first tricycle by Edoardo Bianchi, motorcycle manufacturing in Italy became widespread. This development was no doubt helped by the geographical proximity of the French, the great innovators in the field of motor sport and manufacturing.

The first motorcycles to appear in Italy in large numbers were the Hildebrand and Wolfmuller which were sold by the Max Trukeiner organization of Milan around 1895. Immediately afterwards the great American names like Indian, Harley-Davidson, ACE, Excelsior and Henderson took the lead.

At the beginning of the century Italian firms began to appear on the scene: Bianchi, Prinetti & Stucchi, Marchand of Piacenza and Borgo of Turin. There was also the great Frera, of course, which was perhaps the best organized of all Italian motorcycle makers in this period.

The Italian producers were able to turn out relatively powerful machines while at the same time having medium-sized cubic capacities. By contrast

After the war, racing became popular again. New makers entered the scene hoping to capture the attentions of an ever increasing public. Here we see apart from the already established MOTO GUZZI the new MV AUGUSTA.

the Americans made enormous machines of 1000 cc or more, adopting the classic arrangement of twin "V" cyclinders or else using a four cylinder in-line engine. After years of struggling both on the track and on the market, Itallan small and medium cylinder machines finally showed their superiority in economic and technical terms. It is from this moment that the Italian motorcycle industry really takes off and Moto Guzzi in particular, which began in 1920, immediately gained success on the market.

In the fifties, the victories in sporting competitions achieved by Bianchi, Guzzi and Gilera, their world records and their high quality mass produced motorcycles, which were popular among all classes of people, raised the Italian motorcycle industry to a position of pre-eminence on the international scene.

The sidecar reaches its height in the fifties. The passenger travels comfortably in a little cockpit.

*Two HARLEY
DAVIDSON, Sport
Starter 883.
A legendary
motorcycle, the
dream of every
motorcycle
enthusiast.*

The United States

The United States occupies a pre-eminent position in the history of the motorcycle industry. Strange though it may seem, this is especially true of the development of motorcycle racing in Europe, from its beginnings to the first written regulations.

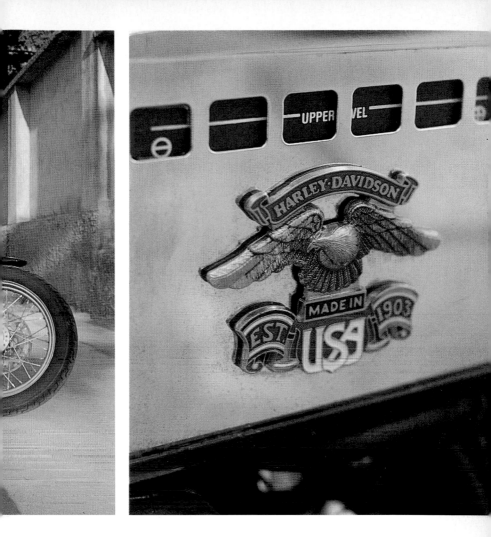

Indeed, the Americans produced the first big machines that braved the improvised circuits on the old continent and stimulated the local manufacturers to catch up. In this way the Europeans sought new and ever more refined solutions to technical problems as firms tried to improve on the American models.

At the beginning of the century Indian and

All makers produced shaped fuel tanks with fairings. Here we see the Italian MV AUGUSTA and MONDIAL.

Harley-Davidson created the twin in-line "V" engine, while ACE and Henderson followed the current fashion in the motor car industry and built motorcycles with powerful four cylinder in-line engines.

In 1913 as many as seventy thousand machines were produced in America, a good many of these being exported to Europe. But after the first world war the market in Europe for American made cycles began to decline. One reason for this

was the increasing popularity of the motor car after the arrival of Henry Ford's Model "T". Then in England, Italy and Germany motorcycle racers who had once relied on Indians or Harley-Davidsons began to prefer the powerful but more manageable Nortons, AJSs or Velocettes. The American motorcycle industry no longer competed on the international racing scene and focused instead on the domestic market. Motorcycle racing in America consequently developed in its

RUMI 175 cc, SPORT, 1953. The Bergamo based firm began producing motorcycles in 1949.

SCHEMA INTERNO DELLA VESPA 150 cc.

own way, following the public taste for highly spectacular displays in which the main features were the power and speed of the machines rather than the riding skill and athletic prowess of the racers.

It was only towards the beginning of the seventies that the situation began to change in America, partly because of what the Japanese had achieved in motorcycle racing, and there was a revived interest in what was happening elsewhere. The 200 Mile Dayton race had been dominated for years by ancient Harley-Davidson machines and was only of local interest. But when the first European racers began to take part, the race was suddenly raised to a level of world importance.

Japan

After the second world war Japan was completely destroyed as a military and economic power. With the patience typical of orientals, the Japanese began their programme of industrial reconstruction, aiming to continue the ambitions which had been interrupted by the war.

This time, however, there was no longer an emphasis on the military strength and the lust for conquest that had led Japan to ruin. The country had brains and a desire to get on with work. At the same time Japan wanted to be counted among the great powers of the world. In order to do this in peace

Today the motorcycle for use in town takes on new forms resembling those of the scooter.

A modern scooter, the AMICO, produced by the Italian firm APRILIA.

In the seventies racing reached the height of its popularity with English and Italian riders fighting it out for supremacy.

time it was necessary to build up a solid industrial-economic empire. The Japanese began to make everything, in the electronic field from small pocket-sized radios to the most sophisticated electronic components. At the same time they encouraged the development of mechanical engineering, exploiting Western know-how as well as their own war-time experience.

They knew the way the wind was blowing. After the war in Europe and the United States a period of mass motorization began, encouraged by powerful advertising whose maximum expression was the direct participation in car and cycle racing.

Thus the Japanese, after having quietly and carefully got themselves ready to face up to the problems of production on a large scale, officially presented themselves on the European circuits at the beginning of 1959.

Honda was the first Japanese firm to make an impact in the English Tourist Trophy, a race which no important manufacturer could afford to ignore. The

*Monza 1973,
GIACOMO
AGOSTINI and
PASOLINI a few
minutes before
the accident
that cost
Pasolini his life.*

system adopted first by Honda and later by other Japanese makers like Yamaha, Suzuki and Kawasaki was very simple. Before competing in Europe they had sent observers to the most famous European circuits to photograph and study in detail the best tourist and racing motorcycles that were around.

Once they were officially represented in Europe, they had the possibility of getting a much closer look at the engines, frames and the way of managing races of the most important names that for years had dominated the racing circuits of the world. In

addition to this they got to know the top English, German and Italian riders. They were more expert than the Japanese who were trying out their new racing bikes. But the Japanese were underestimated, and this, too, turned out to be to their advantage.

Spain

In Spain there is a fascination with danger and vi-olence. This is shown by the national passion for bull-fighting, which although in decline is still cen-

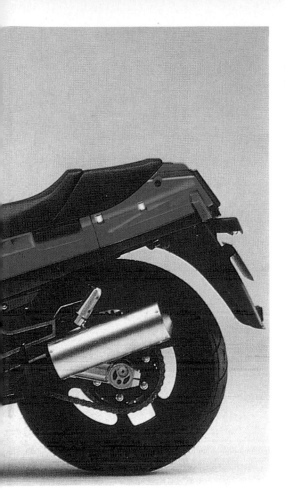

Japanese motorcycles appear as great "beasts" in which the fairings only leave the wheels free. What you can see of the engine conveys the impression of terrific power.

tral to Spanish culture. It is also demonstrated by the fact that the great motor car race which began in the woods of Versailles near Paris in 1903 had Madrid as its final destination, a place where a vast crowd had gathered to watch the arrival of the "crazy" racers.

As is well-known, those racers never arrived in Madrid. But that did not prevent the Spanish from getting excited about motorized transport and all that could be achieved with it.

However, they still had to wait a long time. The Spanish motorcycle makers were the last to appear on the international scene. But this did not mean that they were left behind. Bultaco, Montesa, Derdi and Ossa are currently among the most well-known names around. Sanglas and Mototrans, on the other hand are more active on the domestic market.

The first Spanish racing motorcycle of any note was the Montesa Sprint, which was produced in 1954 and had a two-stroke 125 cc engine. Soon afterwards we saw the first models from Derbi, Ducson and Lube, which began to race small cylinder machines in the world championships in 1962. At the same time Spanish riders began to become known. Their courage and daring often made up for the lack of horsepower of their machines.

Apart from Sanglas, which makes powerful single cylinder four-stroke machines, and Mototrans, which produces under licence from Ducati, all

Spanish motorcycle makers have always opted for two-stroke engines. Both Derbi and Bultaco, while adopting different solutions to technical problems, have achieved considerable international success.

The off-road market provides the Spanish, along with their north European competitors, with a less demanding sport than speed racing, but a more lucrative one in commercial terms. Their models for moto-cross, trial and Alpine riding satisfy the needs of the most demanding riders. In trial competitions Ossa, Bultaco and Montesa have committed themselves to winning the world championships. Trial riding is a delicate sport for which you need steady nerves, balance and strong bikes with soft suspension and steady but powerful engines working on a low rev count. In this specific area, the Spanish are supreme and regularly beat the motorcycles produced by the big Japanese makers who have been competing for some years now in this specialized market.

Machines for all kinds of use, from touring to off-road motorcycling.
The motorcycle is no longer a practical vehicle for those who cannot afford a car, but a sophisticated machine for amusement and leisure.